D0590480

HIDE AND SEEK
FARM

A Dorling Kindersley Book

Notes for parents

Hide and Seek Farm is a wonderful picture book for you and your child to share. From favourite animals and machines to crops and farmyard equipment, it's filled with all sorts of interesting things to find and talk about. Every page provides lots of I-spy fun, and as children play, they build vocabulary, learn colours, practise counting, and develop observation skills.

To get the most out of this book

● Talk about all the things you can see on each page. Point to the objects, say their names, then hunt for each one together. As children become familiar with the book, they will be able to name and find the objects themselves.

● Encourage your child to describe the different things. What colour or shape are they? What are they made of? What are they used for? Which one does your child like best? Has your child seen the animals and objects at a children's farm?

● Read the rhymes and let your child say them with you. Then help your child find the objects in the rhymes.

● Once your child knows letter sounds, you can play traditional I-spy. Ask your child to spot an object on the page that begins with a certain letter.

Written by Dawn Sirett
Designed by Rachael Parfitt Hunt and Victoria Palastanga
Illustrations by Angela Muss
Additional Illustrations by Rachael Parfitt
Special Additional Photography by Dave
Production Controller Danielle Smith
Production Editor Jennifer Murray

Coventry Education & Learning Service	
3 8002 01791 141 5	
Askews & Holts	17-Jul-2012
	£7.99

First published in Great Britain in 2012 by ...ng Kindersley Limited, 80 Strand, London WC2R 0RL
A Penguin Company

2 4 6 8 10 9 7 5 3 1
001–181702–June/2012

Copyright © 2012 Dorling Kindersley Limited

...reserved. No part of this publication may be reproduced, ...etrieval system, or transmitted in any form or by any means, ...ic, mechanical, photocopying, recording, or otherwise, ...ut the prior written permission of the copyright owner.

...que record for this book is available from the British Library.

ISBN: 978-1-40937-404-6

...ted and bound in China by Leo Paper Products Ltd

Discover more at **www.dk.com**

Picture Credits
The publisher would like to thank the following for their kind permission to reproduce their photographs:
(Key: a=above; b=below/bottom; c=centre; f=far; l=left; r=right; t=top)

Alamy Images: 18c (courgettes), 19tc, 43cb; blickwinkel / McPHOTO / KPA 1ftl (tangerines), 1fcrb (tangerines), 18cla, 19c (tangerines); blickwinkel / Rose 3tr; Bon Appetit / Buntrock, Gerrit Ltd. 1ftl (potatoes), 1fcrb (potatoes), 19tl (potatoes), 19fbr, 42fcrb, 43fcr; foodfolio 2fcl, 18cl (blueberries), 47fbl; Robert Hudson 3fclb; Louis Laliberte 3fcra (tractor), 15tc, 15crb; Keith Leighton 1tr (cherries), 1ca (cherries), 1clb (cherries), 1bc (cherries), 18fbl; Pixmann 1ftr (lemons), 1fclb (lemons), 19fbl, 46cr; David Wootton 14cra, 15clb. **Alvey and Towers:** 15cra, 17bl, 47tr. **Corbis:** Ken Davies 16fcla, 17cb; Digital Zoo 34cla, 34bc; DLILLC 32cla (flower / l), 32cla (flower / r), 33tc (flower), 33crb (flower); Pat Doyle 1cra (kittens), 1bl (kittens), 24tl (ginger kittens), 25crb (kittens), 26fcrb; Debra Ferguson / AgStock Images 16fcl, 17ftl; Ocean 1ca (cow), 1bc (cow), 4br, 5ftl, 12cl, 13br, 34c, 36cra, 38tl. **Dorling Kindersley:** Barleylands Farm Museum and Animal Centre, Billericay 11cl, 46fcr; Alan Buckingham 42fbr, 43fbr; Museo Gauchesco Ricardo Guiraldes 1tr (rope), 1clb (rope), 24ca, 25tl; Jamie Marshall 24c, 25cra (shovel), 30cra, 31fcl; Lindsey Stock 1tc (string), 1cb (string), 33cb, 35cb; Barnabas Kindersley 9fbl, 40cra, 41fclb; Odds Farm Park, High Wycombe, Bucks 1fcla (cow), 1fbr (cow), 4tr, 4ftr, 5cb, 5crb; Stephen Oliver 37ftl; Stephen Oliver / Appaloosa – Golden Nugget Sally Chaplin 1ftl (horse), 1fcrb (horse), 8tr, 8bl, 32tl, 33fbr (horse), 39cr; Queen's Rangers 24fcr (hatchet), 25ftr; Rough Guides 31ftl, 47fcr; South of England Rare Breeds Centre, Ashford, Kent 3cl, 10fclb, 11tc, 22fcra, 23c; Tablehurst Farm 28fcrb, 29ftr (sausages). **Dreamstime.com:** Randy Harris 8cla (t), 9tr; Bjorn Heller 15cl, 21cra, 34ca, 34clb; Isselee 1fcla (calf), 1fbr (calf), 4bl, 5ca (l), 9fcrb, 22cl, 22fclb, 23cl (kitten), 23ftl, 26crb, 26fclb; Viktoria Makarova 1tc (horse), 1cb (horse), 8clb, 8fbl, 9clb, 9br; Svetlana Mihailova 42fclb, 43fcla; Claudia Steininger 22fbr, 23fcra. **Fotolia:** Anatolii 3cra, 34cl, 34ftr; Eric Isselée 1ftr (goat), 1fclb (goat), 8br, 8fcla (b), 26cl (dog); Tan Kian Khoon 1ftl (butterfly), 1fcra (butterfly), 1fcrb (butterfly), 1fbl (butterfly), 33ftl (butterfly), 33ca (butterfly / r), 33cca (butterfly / r), 33cla (butterfly / r), 33cl (butterfly), 33c (butterfly / r), 33c (butterfly / r), 33clb (butterfly), 33cb (butterfly / b), 33cb (butterfly / t), 33bl (butterfly), 33ftl (butterfly), 33fcra (butterfly / r), 33fcra (butterfly / t), 33fcl (butterfly / b), 33fclb (butterfly / b), 33fclb (butterfly / t), 33fbl (butterfly), 33fbl (butterfly); Harald Lange 8cra, 8cb, 9cr. **Getty Images:** AFP Photo / Francois Nascimbeni 30fcrb, 31fbl, 34crb; AFP Photo / Pierre Andrieu 31tr (horses); Aurora / Aaron Ansarov 30clb, 31fcrb; Cultura / Echo 16bc, 17ftr; DAJ 3ftl, 42fcra, 43ftr; Digital Vision / Alistair Berg 17fcra, 46fclb; Digital Vision / Digital Zoo 1tl (pig), 1crb (pig); Digital Vision / ICHIRO 1tr (calf), 1clb (calf), 5cla (l), 5c (l); Nicholas Eveleigh 28ftr (l), 29fbr (l); Flonline / Beate Zoellner 22crb, 23tr; First Light / Benjamin Rondel 30cla, 31fbr; Flickr / Boston Thek Imagery 16fbl, 17ca; Foodcollection RF 1cla (grapes), 1br (grapes), 19cl (grapes); FoodPix / Paula Hible 28clb, 29br; Gavin Hellier / Robert Harding 16crb, 17bc; Image Source 10bc, 11cr; LOOK / Karl Johaentges 12clb, 13ca (goats); National Geographic / Joel Sartore 22cla, 23ca, 30fbr, 31tl; National Geographic / Pete Mcbride 16cl, 17bc;

Oxford Scientific / Mike Hill 30ftl, 31cra; Photodisc / GK Hart / Vikki Hart 32bl (cow / l), 32bl (cow / r), 32bc (cow / c), 32bc (cow / l), 32bc (cow / r), 32br (cow / l), 32br (cow / r), 32fbr (cow / l), 32fbr (cow / r), 33tl (cow), 33ca (cow), 33cra (cow), 33cl (cow), 33clb (cow), 33cb (cow), 33ftr (cow), 33fcr (cow), 33fcrb (cow); Photodisc / Jules Frazier 10fcla, 11fcra; Photographer's Choice / Diane Macdonald 12cla, 13tl; Photographer's Choice / Mark S. Wexler 13bc; Photographer's Choice / Pam Francis 5cla (r), 5c (r), 21cr (cow), 32cla (pig / l), 32cla (pig / r), 32ca, 33tl (pig), 33ftl (pig), 33fbl (pig); Photographer's Choice / Sam Armstrong 28ftr (r), 29fbr (r); Photographer's Choice / Tom Walker 12bc, 13ca (swans); Photographer's Choice / Wilfried Krecichwost 12cra, 13cr; Photolibrary / DogPhoto.Com 12cr, 13cla (puppies); Photonica / Amy Eckert 12cb, 13bl; Robert Harding World Imagery / Annie Owen 30crb, 31crb; Marc Serota 30ftr, 31fcla; Gerard Sioen / Gamma-Rapho 30fcla, 31tr; StockImage / Frederic Pacorel 30fclb, 31fcra; Stone / Bob Elsdale 1cra (sheep), 1bl (sheep), 1ftl (sheep), 1fcla (sheep), 1fcrb (sheep), 1fbr (sheep), 4c (c), 4c (l), 4cr (b), 4cr (c), 4fcl (c), 4fcl (r), 21tl, 21cla (l), 21cla (r), 26fcla; Stone / Catherine Ledner 5fcr; Stone / Denis Waugh 30tl, 31cr; Stone / Joe Toreno 22fbl, 23crb (donkey); Stone+ / Nicolas Russell 30fcra, 31c; Sudres Jean-Daniel / Hemis.fr 28ftl; Taxi / Tony Evans / Timelapse Library 4cr (l), 32cl (lamb / l), 32cl (lamb / r), 32c (lamb / l), 32c (lamb / r), 33tc (lamb), 33fcr (lamb), 33fclb (lamb), 33fclb (lamb). **iStockphoto:** Alan Egginton 14cla, 15bl. **New Holland UK Ltd:** 2c, 3fcr, 14fcrb, 42tl, 43c. **SuperStock:** Minden Pictures 12c, 13clb. **Warren Photographic Limited:** 2ftl (rooster), 2ftr (pup), 12ca, 13cl, 20ftl (b), 21bl (ducklings), 21bl (mouse), 22fcla, 22fcl, 22fcrb, 23clb (dog), 23cb (goat), 23fbr, 27tc, 32clb (goat / l), 32clb (goat / r), 32cb (goat / c), 32cb (goat / l), 32cb (goat / r), 32crb (goat / l), 32fcrb (goat / r), 33tr (goat), 33cla (goat), 33cra (goat), 33c (goat), 33bc (goat), 33fcla (goat), 33fclb (goat), 34fcla, 35cr, 37cra (stretching).

Jacket images: *Front:* **Alamy Images:** blickwinkel / McPHOTO / KPA cra/ (tangerines); Bon Appetit / Buntrock, Gerrit Ltd. crb/ (potatoes); foodfolio bl/ (blueberries); Louis Laliberte clb/ (tractor); Pixmann tr/ (lemons). **Corbis:** Gehl Company cr/ (loader); Ocean ftl/ (cow). **Dorling Kindersley:** Jamie Marshall Photography cr/ (shovel); Odds Farm Park, High Wycombe, Bucks tc/ (calf), fcra/ Weald and Downland Open Air Museum, Chichester tr/ (coop). **Dreamstime.com:** Bjorn Heller fbr. **Warren Photographic Limited:** bc/ (dog), fbl, ftl/ (lamb). *Back:* **Alamy Images.** blickwinkel / McPHOTO / KPA ftl/ (tangerines); Bon Appetit / Buntrock, Gerrit Ltd. bl/ (potatoes). **Corbis:** Ocecn fcrb. **Dorling Kindersley:** Jamie Marshall Photography fcl/ (shovel). **Fotolia:** Eric Isselée tl/ (dog). **Warren Photographic Limited:** fcra/ (dog), fcr/ (goat). *Spine:* **Alamy Images:** Pixmann (lemons). **Warren Photographic Limited:** (lamb).

All other images © Dorling Kindersley
For further information see: **www.dkimages.com**

a chick

a cow

a horse and foal

a saddle

a tractor with
a bale loader

a pig

Contents

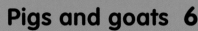

Sheep and cows 4

Pigs and goats 6

Horses and donkeys 8

Farm birds 10

Animal groups 12

Tractors 14

More farm machines 16

Fruit and vegetables 18

Around the farm 20

Noisy farm 22

In the farm shed 24

Mummies and babies 26

At the farm shop 28

Farms around the world 30

Farm counting 32

Look closer 34

Farm silhouettes 36

What goes together? 38

Farm shapes 40

Farm colours 42

Toy farm 44

More to find! 46

Index of words
we've found! 48

a cockerel

an apple

a tractor with a loader

an orange tractor

Boo!

This is
Dotty the Ladybird.
She's on every
page of this book!
See if you can
spot her again
and again.

Sheep and cows

Let's find...

a ewe with 2 lambs

5 black-faced sheep

2 hairy brown cows

4

a black-and-white cow

2 short-haired brown cows

2 brown-and-white calves

a ram

3 pink daisies

3 black-and-white calves

2 milk churns

Baa! Baa!
Moo! Moo!
Spot a black bull
and a black sheep, too.

5

Pigs and goats

Let's find...

3 buckets

2 kids

a brown
nanny goat

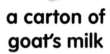
a carton of
goat's milk

some goat's
cheese

a black pig with
a pink stripe

a curly-haired
billy goat

a sow with
6 piglets

a spotty pig

a boar

a pig in a pigsty

6

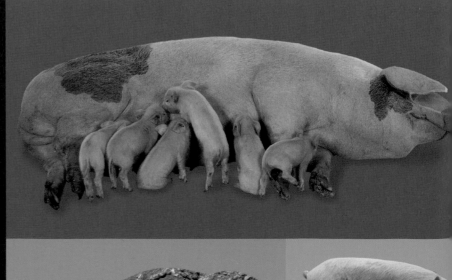

I see a pig's trough
and a shiny goat's bell.
If you can spot them,
you're doing very well.

Horses and donkeys
Let's find...

a horse and cart

a grey horse

6 horseshoes

a donkey carrying a pack

a saddle

2 white shire horses

a chestnut horse

a mare with her foal

a riding hat

a horse and rider

a white horse

a donkey with her foal

a black stallion

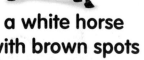

a medal

a white horse with brown spots

8

Find two rosettes,
and read
what they say.
Then choose
who should wear
each rosette today.

Farm birds

Let's find...

5 yellow chicks

a pheasant

a cockerel

a white Aylesbury duck

a duck house

3 geese and 2 goslings

a chick that has just hatched

3 Indian Runner ducks

4 yellow ducklings

a turkey

4 yellow feathers

a brown hen

a guinea fowl

Can you find nine eggs?
I will count them all with you.
Three of them are hatching.
We need to count those, too.

Animal groups

Let's find...

a herd of pigs

a litter of baby rabbits

a herd of cows

a flock of mallard ducks

a herd of deer

a litter of
sheepdog puppies

a herd of goats

a litter of piglets

a flock of sheep

a brood
of ducklings

a gaggle of geese

a clutch
of chicks

A team of five horses
are pulling a plough.
When you can see them,
shout, "Giddy-up now!"

Tractors

Let's find...

a green tractor pulling a blue trailer

a blue
cabless tractor

a red tractor pulling a plough

3 stacked tyres

a green eight-wheeled tractor

5 toy tractors

a red tractor with a loader

a pink tractor

an orange tractor pulling a manure spreader

an old red tractor

Point to the tractor that's lifting a bale of hay. Then choose one busy tractor you'd like to drive today.

More farm machines

Let's find...

a trailer carrying hay bales

an all-terrain vehicle

a pick-up truck

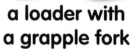
a loader with
a grapple fork

a combine harvester

a crop-spraying plane

a skid-steer loader

an off-road
vehicle

a logging truck

a horsebox

a rice harvester

a grape harvester

a baler

Where is the milk tanker?
Do you know?
With milk from the dairy,
it's ready to go!

Fruit and vegetables

Let's find...

3 slices of cucumber

a box of oranges

2 corn on the cobs

7 apples

a slice of watermelon

6 mushrooms

a pumpkin

18

5 carrots

4 strawberries

an onion

a tray of
courgettes

a lettuce

a sack of
potatoes

a bunch of
bananas

5 tomatoes

I spy some fruit
for our lunch,
red cherries
in a basket
and green grapes
in a bunch.

Around the farm

Let's find...

3 mice

a scarecrow

2 doves

a snail

a squirrel

a frog

2 ducks

a beehive

a sheepdog

a black cat

an owl

2 rabbits

3 sunflowers

3 cygnets

a fence

Where are
the foxes?
Can you see?
Count them with me.
There are three.

Noisy farm

Let's find the noise each animal makes,
then say the funny noises together.

a cockerel goes…   **a mouse goes…**   **a chick goes…**   **a frog goes…**   **a goose goes…**

a sheepdog goes…   **a kitten goes…**   **an owl goes…**   **a duck goes…**

a cow goes…   **a pig goes…**   **a lamb goes…**   **a goat goes…**

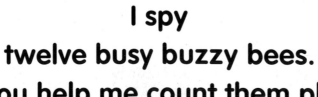 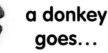 

a donkey goes…   **a horse goes…**

**I spy
twelve busy buzzy bees.
Can you help me count them please?**

22

baaaa!

quack! quack!

squeak! squeak!

neigh!

meow!

cheep! cheep!

cooo! cooo!

oink! oink!

ribbit! ribbit!

naaa!

cock-a-doodle-doo!

23

In the farm shed

Let's find...

a sack

2 cats and
3 kittens

a pair of goggles

2 pairs of gloves

a crate of herbs

a basket of logs

a bucket

a rope

a pair of
ear protectors

a toolbox

a saw

a spanner

a fork

a shovel

a spade

a rake

an axe

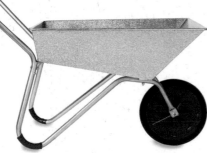
a wheelbarrow

I see three pairs of wellies.
Can you find them all?
Two pairs are big,
and the third is very small.

a broom

Mummies and babies

Let's find the baby that belongs to each mummy animal.

a sheep

a pig

a goat

a chicken

an owl

a rabbit

a sheepdog

a cat

a donkey

a fox

a goose

a cow

a horse

There are seven
yellow ducklings
waddling around.
When you've
found them all,
make a noisy
quack, quack sound!

At the farm shop

Let's find...

a string of garlic

2 bunches of herbs

an apple tart

2 big bottles
of milk

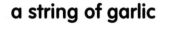

a block of butter

2 bags of flour

a wedge
of cheese

a loaf of bread

2 jars of strawberry jam

a tub of muesli

3 pots
of yoghurt

3 bottles of
apple juice

6 eggs in a carton

a jar
of biscuits

some strings
of sausages

I spy something sweet and runny,
a jar of golden, sticky honey.

28

Farms around the world

Let's find...

a flower farm

a tea plantation

a salmon farm

a sugar cane plantation

a coconut plantation

an apple orchard

a rice farm

a cattle ranch

a cotton plantation

a bee farm

a banana plantation

a chilli pepper farm

a vineyard

a coffee plantation

What more can we find
on our I-spy trail?
Three horses
on a stud farm.
That's where horses
are for sale.

a bison ranch

30

Farm counting

Let's find...

1 horse

2 flowers

3 piglets

4 lambs

5 chickens

6 chilli peppers

7 goats

8 lettuces

9 cows

10 strawberries

I spy twenty
fluttery things.
They're butterflies
with blue-and-white wings.

32

Look closer

a pig

Let's find a close-up of...

 a sheepdog

 a sheep

 a tractor

 a corn on the cob

 some wheat

34

a strawberry

a mallard
duck

a slice
of orange

a sunflower

a wellie boot

a frog

a cat

a reel of string

a cockerel

Now look at these pages
one more time,
and count the crickets.
There are nine!

Farm silhouettes

Let's find silhouettes of...

a flower

4 pears

3 ducklings

a hay bale

2 bananas

a cow

a calf

36

a chick

a sheepdog

3 snails

a watering can

a rabbit

a basket
of eggs

a lamb

a tractor

3 kittens

2 pots
of yoghurt

I spy a silhouette
that goes
cock-a-doodle-doo!
How quickly
can you find it, too?

What goes together?

Let's work out which things go together by following the dotted lines.

Cows give us…

flour

Wheat is ground up to make…

strawberry jam

Strawberries are used to make…

milk

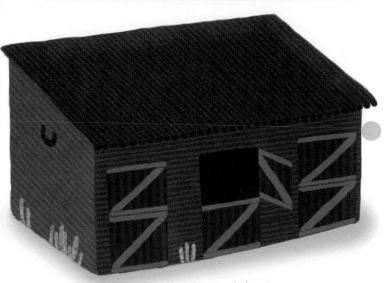

A stable is
a home for a…

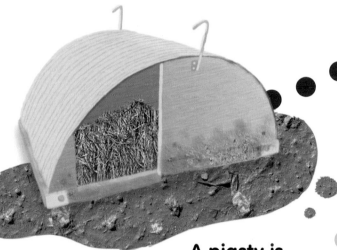

A pigsty is
a home for a…

A chicken coop is
a home for a…

chicken

horse

pig

Find two little chicks.
They look very sweet.
What are they saying?
Chirpy cheep cheep!

39

Farm shapes

Let's find...

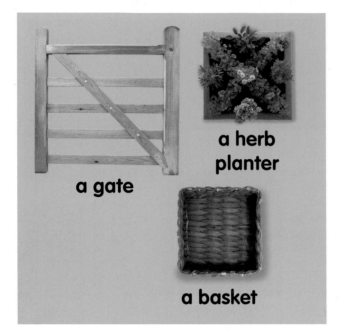

a gate

a herb planter

a basket

squares

a food trough

a fence

a crate of tomatoes

rectangles

a sunflower

a nest

an apple

circles

3 olives

an egg

a lemon

ovals

a duck house   a wedge of cheese

triangles

I spy a slice of starfruit.
It's the shape of a star.
Can you see this fruit?
You won't need
to look far.

41

Farm colours

Let's find...

a yellow sunflower

a blue tractor

a pair of red wellies

3 green leaves

2 pink piglets

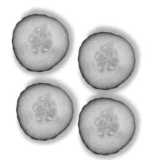

4 green slices
of cucumber

a black tyre

2 white lambs

a yellow chick

a brown foal

an orange slice
of orange

a silver bucket

an orange
carrot

a brown sack
of brown potatoes

a bunch of
green grapes

a brown hen

a blue
watering can

a red strawberry

a purple plum

I can see twelve rainbows,
beautiful and bright.
Let's count them all.
What a colourful sight!

Toy farm

Let's find...

3 horses

a cockerel

2 tractors

an owl

a swan

a bucket

a black sheep

44

a pig and 3 piglets

a mallard duck

3 frogs

a kennel

a dog with a collar

4 butterflies

2 farmers

a cow

There are five kitty cats for you to seek. Point to the one you would like to keep.

More to find!

You'll find all these things if you go back and look at the big, busy pictures in this hide-and-seek book!

3 flowers in a pot

a bath duck

2 crates of potatoes

a jar of marmalade

a broccoli floret

a box of lemons

2 chickens at a chicken feeder

a forklift truck

a sleeping toy dog

half a coconut

a hammer

4 kiwi fruits

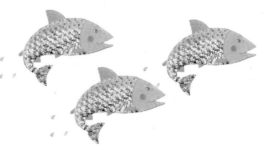

3 leaping salmon

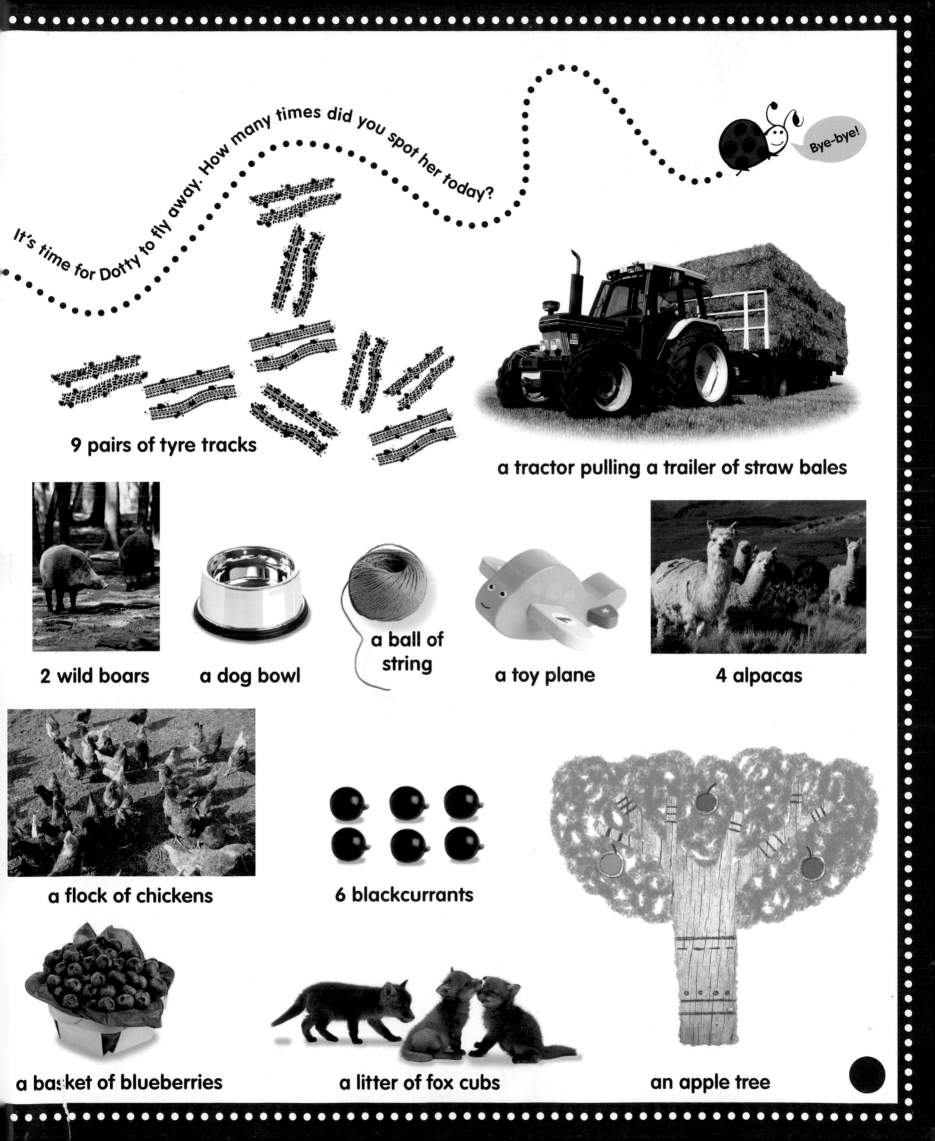

It's time for Dotty to fly away. How many times did you spot her today?

Bye-bye!

9 pairs of tyre tracks

a tractor pulling a trailer of straw bales

2 wild boars

a dog bowl

a ball of string

a toy plane

4 alpacas

a flock of chickens

6 blackcurrants

a basket of blueberries

a litter of fox cubs

an apple tree

Index of words we've found!

all-terrain vehicle 16
alpacas 31, 47
animal group names 12–13, 47
animal homes 6, 10, 20, 31, 39, 40, 45
animal noises 5, 22–23, 27, 37, 39
apple juice 28
apple orchard 30
apples 3, 18, 30, 40, 47
apple tart 28
apple trees 4, 47
axe 24
Aylesbury ducks 10, 20

baby animals 3, 4, 5, 6, 10, 12, 20, 22, 26–27, 32, 36, 37, 39, 42, 45
baby rabbits 12, 27
bags of flour 28, 38
bale loader 3
baler 16
balls of string 25, 47
banana plantation 30
bananas 19, 30, 36
basket of blueberries 18, 47
basket of cherries 18, 19
basket of eggs 37
basket of logs 24
baskets 18, 19, 24, 37, 40, 47
bath ducks 45, 46
bee farm 30
beehive 20
bees 20, 22, 23, 30
bell 7
billy goat 6
birds 3, 10–11, 12, 20, 22, 26, 27, 32, 35, 36, 37, 39, 42, 44, 45, 46, 47
biscuits 28
bison ranch 30
black-and-white calves 5
black-and-white cows 5, 12, 22, 32, 36, 38
black bull 4, 5
black cat 20
blackcurrants 41, 47
black-faced sheep 4
black pig with a pink stripe 6
black sheep 5, 44
black stallion 8
black tyres 14, 42
block of butter 28
blue-and-white butterflies 32
blueberries 18, 47
blue cabless tractor 14
blue tractors 14, 42, 44, 47
blue trailer 14
blue watering can 42
boar (male pig) 6
boars (wild) 31, 47
boots 24, 25, 35, 42
bottles of apple juice 28
bottles of milk 28
box of lemons 19, 46
box of oranges 18
bread 28
broccoli florets 18, 46
brood of ducklings 12
broom 24
brown-and-white calves 5, 27, 36
brown cows 4, 5, 26
brown foals 3, 8, 27, 42

brown hens 10, 26, 32, 39, 42, 47
brown nanny goats 6, 22, 26, 32
brown sack of brown potatoes 19, 42
buckets 6, 24, 42, 44
bull 4, 5
bunches of herbs 28
bunch of bananas 19
bunch of green grapes 18, 19, 42
butter 28
butterflies 32, 33, 45

Cabless tractor 14
calves 5, 27, 36
carrots 19, 42
cart 8
carton of goat's milk 6
carton of milk (cow's) 28
cats and kittens 20, 24, 26, 35, 44, 45
cattle 3, 4–5, 12, 22, 26, 27, 30, 32, 36, 38, 45
cattle ranch 30
cheese 6, 28, 40
cherries 18, 19
chestnut horse 8
chicken coop 39
chicken feeder 46
chickens and chicks 10, 11, 13, 26, 32, 39, 42, 46, 47
chickens at a chicken feeder 11, 46
chicks 3, 10, 12, 22, 26, 37, 39, 42
chick that has just hatched 10
chilli pepper farm 30
chilli peppers 30, 32
circles 40
close-ups 34–35
clutch of chicks 12
cockerels 3, 10, 22, 35, 36, 37, 44
coconut plantation 30
coconuts 30, 41, 46
coffee plantation 30
combine harvester 16
corn on the cobs 18, 34
cotton plantation 30
counting from one to ten 32–33
courgettes 19
cows and calves 3, 4–5, 12, 22, 26, 27, 30, 32, 36, 38, 45
crate of herbs 24
crate of tomatoes 40
crates of potatoes 44, 46
crickets 34, 35
crop-spraying plane 16
cucumber 18, 42
curly-haired billy goat 6
cygnets 20

dairy 16
daisies 5
deer 12
dog bowls 44, 47
dogs and puppies 12, 20, 22, 26, 27, 34, 37, 44, 45, 46
dog with a collar 45
donkey carrying a pack 8
donkey foals 8, 26
donkeys and donkey foals 8–9, 22, 26
doves 20
duck houses 10, 40
ducklings 10, 12, 26, 27, 36
ducks and ducklings 10, 12, 20, 22, 35, 45, 46

ear protectors 24
eggs 10, 11, 28, 37, 40
eggs in a carton 10, 11, 28
eight-wheeled tractor 14
ewes and lambs 4, 12, 26, 27, 34

farmers 45
farms around the world 30–31
farm shop 28–29
feathers 10
fences 20, 40
fish 30, 31, 46
flock of chickens 13, 47
flock of mallard ducks 12
flock of sheep 12
flour 28, 38
flower farm 30
flowers 5, 20, 25, 30, 32, 35, 36, 40, 42, 46
flowers in a pot 25, 46
foals 3, 8, 26, 27, 42
food 6, 10, 11, 18–19, 24, 28–29, 30, 32, 34, 35, 36, 37, 38, 40, 42, 46, 47
food troughs 6, 7, 40
fork 24
forklift trucks 17, 46
fox cubs 13, 26, 47
foxes and fox cubs 13, 20, 21, 26, 47
frogs 20, 22, 35, 45
fruit 3, 18–19, 30, 32, 35, 36, 38, 40, 41, 46, 47

gaggle of geese 12
garlic 28
gate 40
geese and goslings 10, 12, 22, 26
gloves 24
goats and kids 6–7, 12, 22, 26, 27, 32
goat's bell 7
goat's cheese 6
goat's milk 6
goggles 24
goose 10, 12, 22, 26
goslings 10, 26
grape harvester 16
grapes 18, 19, 30, 42
grapple fork 16
green eight-wheeled tractor 14
green grapes in a bunch 18, 19, 42
green leaves 42
green slices of cucumber 42
green tractor pulling a blue trailer 14
green tractors 3, 14
grey horse 8
guinea fowl 10

hairy brown cows 4
half a coconut 41, 46
hammers 25, 46
hatching eggs 10, 11
hay bales 15, 16, 36
hens and chicks 10, 11, 13, 26, 32, 39, 42, 46, 47
herb planter 40
herbs 24, 28, 40
herd of cows 12
herd of deer 12
herd of goats 12
herd of pigs 12
honey 28, 29
horse and cart 8
horse and rider 8

horsebox 16
horses and foals 3, 8–9, 13, 22, 26, 27, 30, 31, 32, 39, 42, 44
horseshoes 8

Indian Runner ducks 10

jar of biscuits 28
jar of honey 28, 29
jar of marmalade 29, 46
jars of strawberry jam 28, 38

kennel 45
kids 6, 27
kittens 22, 24, 26, 37
kitty cats 44, 45
kiwi fruits 41, 46

lambs 4, 22, 27, 32, 37, 42
leaping salmon 31, 46
leaves 42
lemons 19, 40, 46
lettuces 19, 32
litter of baby rabbits 12
litter of fox cubs 13, 47
litter of piglets 12
litter of puppies 12
litter of rabbits 12
litter of sheepdog puppies 12
loaders 3, 15, 16
loader with a grapple fork 16
loaf of bread 28
logging truck 16
logs 24

machines 3, 14–17, 34, 37, 42, 44, 46, 47
mallard ducks 12, 22, 35, 45
manure spreader 15
mares and foals 3, 8, 26, 27
marmalade 29, 46
medal 8
mice 20, 22
milk 5, 6, 16, 17, 28, 38
milk churns 5
milk tanker 16, 17
mouse 20
muesli 28
mummy and baby animals (both) 3, 4, 5, 6, 8, 10, 12, 20, 22, 24, 26–27, 32, 36, 37, 39, 42, 45, 47
mushrooms 18

nanny goats and kids 6, 12, 22, 26, 27, 32
nest 40
noises 5, 22–23, 27, 37, 39

Off-road vehicle 16
old red tractor 15
olives 40
onion 19
orange carrots 19, 42
oranges (fruit) 18, 35, 42
orange slices of orange 35, 42
orange tractor pulling a manure spreader 15
orange tractors 3, 15
orchard 30
ovals 40
owlet 27
owls and owlets 20, 22, 26, 27, 44

Pair of ear protectors 24
pair of goggles 24
pair of red wellies 42

pairs of gloves 24
pairs of tyre tracks 17, 47
pairs of wellies 24, 25, 42
pears 36
pheasant 10
pick-up truck 16
pig in a pigsty 6
piglets 6, 12, 26, 32, 42, 45
pigs and piglets 3, 6–7, 12, 22, 26, 34, 39, 45
pigsties 6, 39
pig's trough 6, 7
pink daisies 5
pink piglets 6, 12, 26, 32, 42, 45
pink tractor 15
planes 16, 44, 47
plantations 30
planter 40
ploughs 13, 14
plum 42
potatoes 19, 42, 44, 46
pots of yoghurt 28, 37
puppies 12, 27
purple 42
purple plum 42

rabbits and baby rabbits 12, 20, 26, 27, 37
rabbits (babies) 12, 27
rainbows 42, 43
rake 24
ram 5
ranches 30
rectangles 40
red cherries in a basket 18, 19
red strawberry 42
red tractor pulling a plough 14
red tractors 3, 14, 15, 34, 37, 44
red tractor with a loader 15
reel of string 35
rice farm 30
rice harvester 16
rider 8
riding hat 8
rope 24
rosettes 8, 9

Sack of potatoes 19, 42
sacks 19, 24, 42
saddles 3, 8
salmon 31, 46
salmon farm 30
sausages 28
saw 24
scarecrow 20
shapes 40–41
shed 24–25
sheep and lambs 4–5, 12, 22, 26, 27, 32, 34, 37, 42, 44
sheepdog puppies 12, 27
sheepdogs and puppies 12, 20, 22, 26, 27, 34, 37
shire horses 8
short-haired brown cows 5, 26
shovel 23
silhouettes 36–37
silver bucket 42
skid-steer loader 16
sleeping toy dogs 44, 46
slice of starfruit 40, 41
slice of watermelon 18
slices of cucumber 18, 42
slices of orange 35, 42
snails 20, 37
sows and piglets 6, 26
spade 24

spanner 24
spotty pigs 3, 6, 22, 39
squares 40
squirrel 20
stables 31, 39
stacked tyres 14
stallion 8
star 40, 41
starfruit 40, 41
straw bales 15, 47
strawberries 19, 32, 35, 38, 42
strawberry jam 28, 38
string 25, 35, 47
string of garlic 28
strings of sausages 28
stud farm 30, 31
sugar cane plantation 30
sunflowers 20, 35, 40, 42
swan 44

tanker (milk) 16, 17
team of horses 13
tea plantation 30
tomatoes 19, 40
toolbox 24
tools 24, 25, 46
toy dogs 44, 45, 46
toy planes 44, 47
toys 15, 44–45, 46, 47
toy tractors 15, 44
tractor lifting a hay bale 15
tractor pulling a trailer of straw bales 15, 47
tractors 3, 14–15, 34, 37, 42, 44, 47
tractor with a bale loader 3, 15
tractor with a loader 3, 15
trailer carrying hay bales 16
trailer carrying straw bales 15, 47
trailers 14, 15, 16, 47
tray of courgettes 19
triangles 40
troughs 6, 7, 40
trucks 16, 17, 46
tub of muesli 28
turkey 10
tyres 14, 42
tyre tracks 17, 47

Vegetables 18–19, 32, 46
vehicles 3, 14–17, 34, 37, 42, 44, 46, 47
vineyard 30

Watering cans 37, 42
watermelon 18
wedges of cheese 28, 40
wellie boots 24, 25, 35, 42
wheat 34, 38
wheelbarrow 24
white Aylesbury duck 10, 20
white horse 8
white horse with brown spots 8, 32, 39
white lambs 4, 22, 27, 32, 37, 42
white shire horses 8
wild boars 31, 47
world farms 30–31

yellow chicks 3, 10, 22, 26, 37, 39, 42
yellow ducklings 10, 12, 26, 27, 36
yellow feathers 10
yellow sunflowers 20, 35, 40, 42
yoghurt 28, 37

3 8002 01791 141 5